The New Hat

Will she find a
new hat?

The
New Hat

Paul Shipton
Illustrated by Melanie Mansfield

CW00520979

Walkth

This is

goes sl

Let's rea

Do you think she likes this hat?

Walkthrough

This is the back cover – let's read
the blurb together.

'Will she find a new hat?'

Look at the picture.

What hat is she wearing?

Is it different from the hat on
the front cover?

Walkthrough

This is the title page.

Look at all the hats.

Which hat do you like best?

Read the names of the author,
illustrator and publisher.

Walkthrough

What is happening in the picture?

What has the lady seen?

What is the problem?

 Observe and Prompt

Word Recognition

- Point out the speech bubble and check the children read the text.

- Explain that 'no' is a word that the children will see often in the book. Check they can read this word.

Observe and Prompt

Language Comprehension

- Check the children understand what has happened at the start of the story.

- Ask the children what the lady might say. Why?

- How do the children think she would say it?

- Check the children read the text in the speech bubble with appropriate expression.

Walkthrough

Where is the lady going? (*into the hat shop*)

What does she want? (*a new hat*)

How does she feel?

 Observe and Prompt

Word Recognition

- Check the children can read the words 'I', 'want', 'you' and 'like'. (These are sight words – words likely to be in their store of familiar words.)

- Check the children are reading 'hat' using their decoding skills. Can they sound out and blend h-a-t all through the word?

- The word 'new' will not be decodable for children at this stage. Tell the children this word.

I want a new hat.

4

Walkthrough

What has the shopkeeper got?

What colour is the hat?

What might the shopkeeper be saying to the lady?

> Do you like this green hat?

5

 Observe and Prompt

Language Comprehension

- Check the children understand what is happening in the story now.

- Ask the children what the shopkeeper is doing.

- Check the children are reading with rising intonation at the question mark.

Walkthrough

Does the lady like the green hat?

How can you tell?

 Observe and Prompt

Word Recognition

- If the children have difficulty with the word 'blue', tell them this word and then model the blending of it for them.

Walkthrough

What colour of hat has the shopkeeper got?

What is he asking the lady?

Do you think she will like it?

Do you like this blue hat?

7

Observe and Prompt

Language Comprehension

- Do the children think the lady liked the green hat?
- Ask the children what the shopkeeper is doing now.
- Check the children are reading with expression.

Walkthrough

What is her answer?

Observe and Prompt

Word Recognition

- If the children have
  difficulty with the word
  'orange', ask them if they
  recognise the initial letter
  and sound – 'o'. Then tell
  them the word and
  model the reading of this
  word for them.

Walkthrough

What do you think the shopkeeper is asking?

What do you think the lady is thinking?

Do you like this orange hat?

 Observe and Prompt

Language Comprehension

- Do the children think the lady liked the blue hat?

- Ask the children if the lady is happy.

- Ask the children if the shopkeeper is happy.

- Check the children are reading with expression, taking notice of exclamation marks, bold text and emphasis.

Walkthrough

What does the lady think of the orange hat?

What does she say?

How is she feeling now?

 Observe and Prompt

Word Recognition

- The word 'purple' will not be decodable for children at this stage. Tell the children this word.

Walkthrough

What does the shopkeeper show the lady next?

What colour is it?

What is the lady's friend doing?

Do you like this purple hat?

11

 Observe and Prompt

Language Comprehension

- Ask the children what the lady might be thinking.
- Ask the children if they think the lady will like the purple hat.
- Check the children recognise the characters' feelings.

11

Walkthrough

Does she like this hat?

How do the shopkeeper and the friend feel? Why?

 Observe and Prompt

Word Recognition

- If the children find it difficult to read 'yes', prompt them to check the word again and blend the CVC sounds, from left to right, through the word.

- Check the children can read the words 'love' and 'my'.

Is everyone happy?

I love my new hat.

13

 Observe and Prompt

Language Comprehension

- Ask the children which hat the lady liked.
- Ask the children what the lady and her friend did next.

Walkthrough

What's happened?

What's the matter?

What might happen next?

 Observe and Prompt

Word Recognition

- Check the children are reading both speech bubbles, reading from left to right.

Observe and Prompt

Language Comprehension

- Ask the children what they think is wrong with the lady's hat.

- Do the children think the lady is happy?

- Do the children think her friend is happy?

Walkthrough

What does the lady want now?

What do you think the lady is saying?

How do you think she is saying it?

👁 Observe and Prompt

Language Comprehension

- What do the children think happened at the end of the story?

- Ask the children if anyone is happy.

- Check the children are reading with appropriate expression.